A HACKER'S DICTIONARY

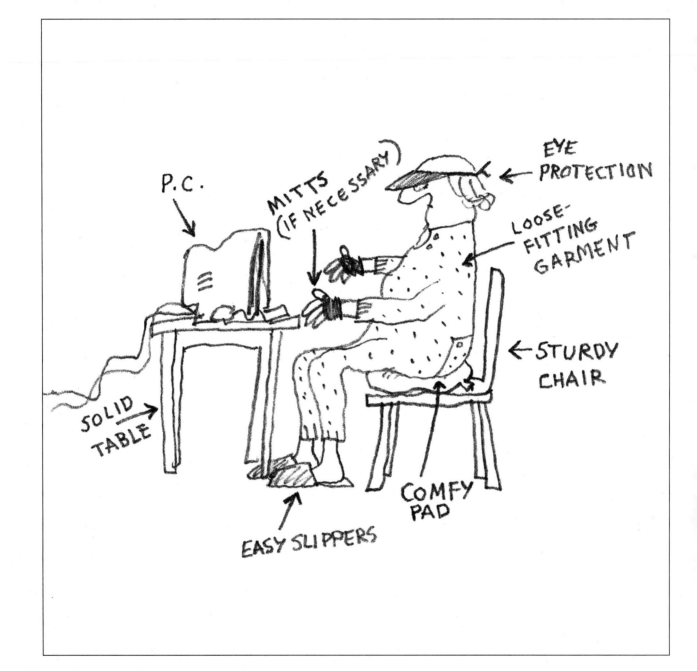

computing

A HACKER'S DICTIONARY

BY HENRY BEARD & ROY McKIE

WORKMAN PUBLISHING
NEW YORK

ACKNOWLEDGMENTS

The author would like to thank the following cybermeisters, propellerheads, technowizards, and turbo gurus for their invaluable assistance: Andy Borowitz, John Boswell, Christopher Cerf, Astrid Cravens, Gwyneth Cravens, Ralph Drumheller, David Gernert, Sally Kovalchick, Jonathan Price, Erik Satre, and Lynn Strong.

Library of Congress Cataloging-in-Publication Data

Beard, Henry.
Com-put-ing: a dictionary for web surfers, number-crunchers, desktop publishers, and space-alien zappers / by Henry Beard & Roy McKie.

p. cm.

ISBN 0-7611-1774-1 (alk. paper)
1. Computers—Dictionaries. I. McKie, Roy. II. Title.
QA76.15 .B39   1999   004'.03—dc21
                                                        CIP

Cover graphics by Linda McCarthy

Workman books are available at special discounts when purchased in bulk for premiums and sales promotions as well as for fund-raising or educational use. For details, contact the Special Sales Director at the address below.

Workman Publishing Company
708 Broadway
New York, New York 10003-9555

Manufactured in the United States of America

First printing November 1999

10   9   8   7   6   5   4   3   2   1

To err is human, but to really screw up you need a computer.

Adventure game

A

....

Access
Entry into an operating system, or connection to a network or the Internet, or any other similar function you could have performed if you hadn't forgotten your password. *See* PASSWORD.

ACK
Code used to **ack**nowledge error-free receipt of transmitted data. Slightly different codes are used to confirm transmission quality but express dissatisfaction with the data itself, including ICK, GAK, UGH, BAH, DOH, and FEH.

Acronym
A word such as BASIC (**B**eginner's **A**ll-purpose **S**ymbolic **I**nstruction **C**ode) that is formed from the initial letters of other words. The word "acronym" is, interestingly enough, itself an acronym that stands for **A C**ompletely **R**idiculous **O**bsolete **N**oun **Y**ou'll **M**isspell.

Active matrix
Advanced liquid crystal computer screen that displays error messages and system failure warnings with exceptional clarity.

Add-on
Any product installed in a computer or attached to a program that boosts its failure rate or expands its capacity for malfunction. *See* UPGRADE.

Address
The specific place in a computer memory where a particular item of data has been lost.

Adventure game
Computer game in which players attempt to follow an incredibly complex path through a series of options. The best-known is 800-MYSTERY, in which callers to a special toll-free number are shunted among dozens of extensions and given bewildering and barely intelligible recorded instructions as they try to obtain technical assistance in loading and operating a completely incomprehensible program. *See* GAMES.

A Hacker's Dictionary

Alert box

A small box that appears on a computer screen to warn you that you are about to do something bad that you didn't have any intention of doing, either because you have no idea of how to do it or you were only doing it in the first place because a previous alert box told you that if you didn't do it, something even worse would happen. *See* CHECK BOX.

Algorithm

A set of instructions that shows how to make it appear that a problem has been solved, transfer responsibility for solving a problem to someone else, or create an entirely new problem.

Align

Command used in word processing that makes data line up horizontally when you want it to line up vertically, and vertically when you want it to line up horizontally.

Alpha testing

The initial phase of testing new software in which highly trained experts on the staff of the manufacturer employ very powerful custom-designed hardware and ingenious temporary fixes to run a specially modified version of the product to find out whether, under absolutely ideal circumstances, the software will perform at approximately one-half its advertised speed or power. *See* BETA TESTING.

Alt

Handy computer control key that makes it possible for a single misdirected finger stroke to create a degree of word-processing chaos formerly achieved only by leaning on the keyboard with both elbows.

America Online

We are sorry, but due to unprecedented reader interest, this extremely amusing definition cannot be accessed at this time.

Ampere

Unit for measuring an electric current, equal to one coulomb per second. Other units commonly used in the computer industry are the Karloff, which measures the destructive strength of a power surge; the Methuselah, which measures

Arrange

promised battery life; and the Gesundheit, which measures actual battery life. *See* BATTERY PACK and OHM'S LAW.

Analog   Method of representing information in which wrong answers or inaccurate readings are expressed as points on a continuous line, rather than as a specific incorrect value. *See* DIGITAL.

Anchor   *1.* Hypertext tag that provides a link to another document. *2.* Possible use for a large and heavy obsolete personal computer.

Apple   Pioneering computer company that, in technical terms, clearly built a better mousetrap, but lost out to competitor Microsoft's more effective long-term strategy of breeding successive generations of worse mice.

Application   Specific task-performing software that can cause blowups, anomalies, and artifacts, as opposed to general operating software, which can cause a system-wide failure. *See* BOMB, CRASH, DOWN, FAIL-SAFE SYSTEM, FRIED, FROZEN, GLITCH, HUNG.

Architecture   *1.* Term often used to refer to the design of a computer system. *2.* Term never used to refer to the design of any building housing a computer company.

Archival storage   External storage system where unneeded data is always available. *See* BACKUP COPY.

Argument   *1.* A value or an option that provides data for a routine. *See* PARAMETER. *2.* Like hell it is. It's a value or an option that modifies a command. *Don't see* PARAMETER; *see* SWITCH. Sheesh.

Arrange   Command that automatically neatens up the columns and rows of document or file icons in a graphical operating system by reorganizing them into the most counterintuitive and least logical possible arrangement.

Arrow keys	A set of four keys that move the cursor too far up, too far down, too far left, or too far right.
Artificial intelligence	*1.* The utilization of computers to simulate human thinking. *2.* Any other simulation of human thinking, such as the thought processes of a typical member of the U.S. Congress. *See* BIONIC.
Audio	Technical term for a sound produced by a computer that isn't immediately followed by a sudden darkening of the screen, the ejection of shards of silicon from the floppy disk slot, or the smell of something burning.
Automatic	Capable of failing without outside input.
Automation	The replacement of a fallible human employee with an unreliable machine.

B

Babbage, Charles	Nineteenth-century inventor of the first true computer, a surprisingly modern mechanical calculating machine that cost twice as much and took four years longer to develop than anticipated, was totally incompatible with every other computational device or method then in existence, and invariably malfunctioned whenever it was demonstrated in public.
Backup copy	A missing disk or tape that contains lost data.
Backward compatibility	The ability of a new and improved model of hardware or an advanced or upgraded software product to run older components and earlier versions that actually work. *See* UPWARD COMPATIBLE.

Backup copy

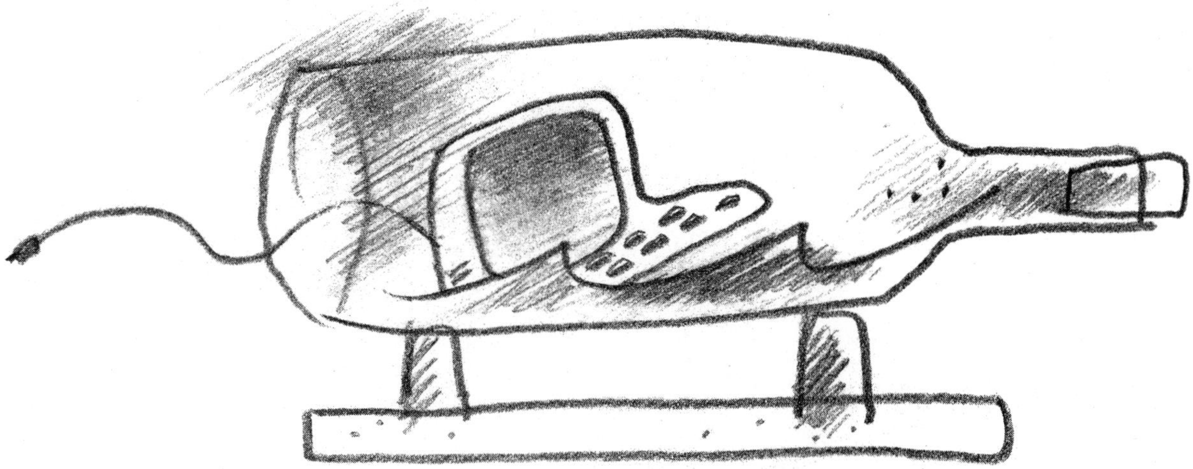

Bar code

A Hacker's Dictionary

Bandwidth

1. The carrying capacity of any communications system. *2.* The word "sandwich" as typed out by voice recognition software.

Bar code

A pattern of thin vertical stripes printed on a product package that makes it possible for a supermarket checkout clerk to whisk your jumbo jar of Chef Boyardee Spaghetti Sauce over an optical scanner, instantly charging you $4.89 for a container of chèvre cheese and simultaneously informing inventory control that it is time to order a fully loaded Chevy Suburban.

BASIC

Acronym for **B**eginner's **A**ll-purpose **S**ymbolic **I**nstruction **C**ode, one of the earliest high-level programming languages, which Bill Gates adapted for use in Microsoft's Disk Operating System (MS-DOS) primarily because BASIC makes it very easy to program simple calculations quickly, like determining how many billions of dollars someone could make if 90% of all the PCs in the world had to use his software.

Batch processing

A mode of computer operation in which a large number of completed transactions are processed all at once, as, for example, when a bank sends out several thousand inaccurate monthly balances, as opposed to an on-line, real-time processing method in which a database is constantly updated as transactions occur, and improper charges, unwarranted deductions, and misplaced deposits are entered continuously.

BAT file

1. Short for "batch file," the name used in DOS systems for a file that contains a number of consecutive commands. *2.* Data stored in the computer in the Batcave, like Bruce Wayne's tax returns, the Rolodex for the Batphone, the lease-payment schedule on the Batmobile, and the household inventory for stately Wayne Manor.

A Hacker's Dictionary

Battery pack
A rechargeable source of electricity used in portable notebook computers which, depending on the type of battery technology employed and the capacity of the individual unit, provides anywhere from one-half to two-thirds of the minimum power needed to complete any significant task.

Bay
A site in a personal computer case or cabinet where a disk or tape drive can be installed by a user, generally in under 10 hours and usually with ordinary household tools no more complex or specialized than a ballpoint pen, a letter opener, a corkscrew, an ice pick, and a set of fireplace tongs.

Benchmark
1. A type of comparison test of hardware or software typically undertaken by editors at computer industry trade magazines. 2. Visible indication of an overnight stay on a park bench left by an out-of-work computer magazine editor who gave a poor rating to an Intel chip or a piece of Microsoft software.

Bernoulli box
Very fast eight-inch disk drive with a large storage capacity based on an aerodynamic principle discovered by an 18th-century Swiss scientist. Now obsolete, the Bernoulli drive's chief advantage was that when it failed, the enraged computer user could fling it Frisbee-style nearly half a mile.

Beta testing
A second level of software testing in which copies of a nearly finished, almost market-ready product are distributed to a limited number of carefully selected, exceptionally knowledgeable volunteers with advanced degrees in computer science to see if they can load the program in less than one week and get it to run properly at least a third of the time.

Bin
1. Common directory name for a binary file where executable programs are placed. 2. Common descriptive name for a padded cell where certifiable ex-programmers are placed.

Beta testing

Blank character

A Hacker's Dictionary

Binary   A base-2 numbering system with only two digits, 0 and 1, which is perfectly suited for electronic operations since it can be expressed by power states (on/off), voltage levels (high/low), or charge (positive/negative), but is less than ideal for humans, who find it awkward to say things like "It's a Catch-10110 situation," "He's the 11011010-pound gorilla," and "That's the 10110010011011001-dollar question."

Bind   1. (v.) To assign an address to a symbolic reference or a value or type to a variable parameter. 2. (v.) To link drivers together for network communications. 3. (n.) A situation computer users find themselves in when symbolic addresses fail to respond to instructions, the initialized variables display the wrong parameters, or the drivers turn out to be incompatible.

Bionic   1. Descriptive term for a machine designed using a human pattern, like the leaf blower, which was originally based on Pat Buchanan. 2. Descriptive term for an artificial replacement for a human body part that far exceeds normal human capabilities, such as Sam Donaldson's toupee. *See* ROBOT.

Bit   Shorthand for **binary digit**, the smallest possible unit of computer misinformation, which has one of only two values: 0 if it should have been 1, and 1 if it should have been 0. *See* BYTE.

Blank character   1. A one-byte character representing the linear interval produced by a single press of the keyboard space bar. 2. Personality type sought by the personnel department of the Microsoft Corporation.

Block   1. A group of characters, records, or other data that is stored, transferred, copied, saved, or transmitted as a unit. 2. A temporary inability on the part of a writer to come up with anything even remotely funny in a term like "block."

BNC

Abbreviation for **B**ritish **N**aval **C**onnector, a widely used, bayonet-style coaxial cable connector originally designed for the wireless set on the *Titanic*. To join two sections of cable, a flimsy tin pin in the center of a thin metal tube on the male end is jammed blindly into a circular socket with a microscopic center hole on the female end, and then a rotating ring around the male end is tightened until its threads are stripped, bending the pin against the buffer surrounding the center hole and mashing the metal tube, thus ensuring that no contact whatsoever is made. *See* CABLE MODEM.

Bold

A heavier-than-normal typeface that can be selected in most word-processing programs, but may not be reproduced satisfactorily by cheap printers which have default settings for different type weights, like "fuzz," "murk," "blur," "smear," "blob," and "glop." *See* PRINTER.

Bomb

Slang term for "fail," usually referring to a program failure. Software manufacturers prefer more formal descriptions of this event, such as "The program experienced a sudden short-term success deficit," "The program shifted into an active-status zero-productivity mode," "The program entered a temporary nonfunctional operational state," or "The program exhibited a significantly disenhanced performance-capability profile."

Boolean logic

Binary-number algebraic system developed by the 19th-century mathematician George Boole in which all values are either True or False, and AND, OR, and NOT are the primary operations. It has been supplanted recently by the system of Billean logic developed by the 20-century politician Bill Clinton, in which values can be True, Sort of True, Not Entirely True, True but Misleading, and A Little False, and the primary operations are BUT, MAYBE, IF, and SO? *See* FUZZY LOGIC.

Bug

A Hacker's Dictionary

Boot
1. To load the operating system software that starts a computer. *2.* After loading the operating system software and waiting a decent interval during which a computer fails to start, to deliver a sharp kick to the cabinet of a mainframe computer, or to hit the side of a desktop computer with a shoe, or to dropkick a laptop computer across a room.

Box
1. In a graphical user interface, a bordered area in which information is presented. *2.* A cardboard container the size of a truck in which an electronic component no larger than a domino is packed.

BPS
Bits **p**er **s**econd, a measure of the speed at which data is transmitted. Because of the undercapacity of many Internet service providers, compatibility problems in office communications systems, and bandwidth limitations in phone lines, many senders prefer to use more practical measures, like e-mails per gigajiffy, memos per millimonth, and faxes per fortnight.

Buffer
A place where data is temporarily held prior to being accidentally erased or inadvertently deleted.

Bug
An unplanned troublesome characteristic of a program, as opposed to an irritating feature that was consciously designed or deliberately included.

Bundle
1. (v.) To package software that customers do not want with a computer or another program they do want. *2. (n.)* What software publishers make as a result of pursuing this innovative marketing strategy.

Bus
A set of parallel electronic connections designed to pick up data that has been hanging around the terminal playing video games and accessing dirty web pages on the Internet, and take it over to the Central Processing Unit for a good talking-to.

Button

A small click-activated circle or bar in a dialog box that allows a computer user to select an ill-advised option or issue an improper command.

Byte

Shorthand for binary term, a unit of computer memory composed of 8 bits, or enough to produce a single mistyped alphanumeric character. A minimum of 16 bits is required for the simplest typographical error; 32 bits are needed for more complex letter transpositions; 64 bits are necessary for even the most minor spelling mistake; a fully garbled word comprises no less than 256 bits; and a completely indecipherable paragraph could easily consume several thousand bits, or kilobits. *See* MEGABYTE *and* MEMORY.

C

Cable

An insulated bundle of wires of insufficient length or inadequate capacity with a nonstandard connector at either end.

Cable modem

An Internet connection device that permits cable-TV subscribers to send threatening e-mail to Barney, get health tips from Dr. Quinn, Medicine Woman, order merchandise from Beverly Hills 90210, download the X-files, and make reservations on Gilligan's Island.

Cache

A special high-speed memory bank that allows frequently or recently used data to be accessed very quickly, thus dramatically decreasing the time between crashes.

Calculator

Handy, portable, palm-sized substitute for eight years of straight A's in math.

Camera-ready copy

Text or artwork in a final state of preparation prior to being misprinted.

Cell phone

Carpal tunnel syndrome A repetitive strain injury producing pain and tingling in the fingers and wrist caused by prolonged use of computer keyboards. A less well-publicized but equally serious condition is Aural Funnel Syndrome, a numbness in the neck and general dizziness caused by having recorded music played into your ear at high volume from a phone wedged between your shoulder and your chin while waiting on hold for technical support.

Carriage Paper-feeding printer mechanism that at the exact midpoint of a critical, deadline-sensitive document printout, suddenly turns into a pumpkin. *See* PRINTER.

Cathode ray tube Vacuum-tube video terminal found in most desktop computers. CRTs, as they are known, are bulkier and somewhat harder on the eyes than the Liquid Crystal Display (LCD) panels used in laptops, but on the plus side a burnt-out video monitor can, with a little ingenuity, be converted into a handsome aquarium, while defunct flat-screen laptops can really only be recycled as trivets, leaf or flower presses, or home plate on a baseball diamond.

CD-ROM Compact Disc Read-Only Memory, an optical disk that can hold up to 680 megabytes of data—enough memory to store every single book an average individual is never going to get around to reading in an entire lifetime.

Cell Place in a spreadsheet application where, because you were found guilty of an illegal operation, your computer decided to lock up your data and throw away the key.

Cell phone Key component in a voluntary but widely honored international identity system in which an individual publicly displays a small handheld communicator that warns everyone in the immediate vicinity that the person in question is a jerk.

A Hacker's Dictionary

Central processing unit

The single integrated chip that acts as the "brains" of a personal computer, planning the next "job" and "rubbing out" any data that gets in the way.

Chaos

A theory proposed by the mathematician Benoit Mandelbrot that holds that the apparent disorder of the universe is not disorder at all, but a hidden type of fractal-based order, and that consequently the Big Bang is not covered by the warranty.

Character

Any letter, number, punctuation mark, or symbol found on or accessed by a computer keyboard. Characters can be visible, like "A," "9," "!," or "@," or invisible, like "   ," "   ," "   ," and "   ."

Chat room

On-line, real-time electronics forum which, in a miracle of modern Internet communications, permits many users at separate locations often hundreds or even thousands of miles apart to simultaneously bore each other to death.

Check box

A dialog box in which a user is permitted to select from among a list of irrelevant or inapplicable options instead of being forced to choose between two unpalatable alternatives.

Chip

A wafer of silicon or some other semiconductor containing a miniaturized integrated circuit with as much processing power as a '70s-era mainframe computer, or, to put it another way, the same capacity for error as an entire regional IRS tax office during the Carter administration.

Circuit board

A flat silicon sheet on which electronic components are located. The two primary types found in computers are the "motherboard," which contains the central processing unit, memory, and controllers, and the "daughtercards," which provide expansion capacity. Unfortunately, many computers are manufactured with cheaper and less reliable circuit boards,

CENTRAL PROCESSING UNIT

TURKEY PLATTER UNIT

Command

including the conflict-prone mother-in-lawboard, the low-resolution drunken-uncleboard, the logic-stressed crazy-auntboard, the troublesome evil-stepsistercard, and the crash-prone smartass brothercard.

Clear

1. (n.) Command that erases or deletes data. *2. (adj.)* What the instruction manual obviously was not, or you never would have selected "clear" to neaten up the appearance of the just-completed text on your screen.

Click

To press and quickly release a mouse button, an action which, because you were not paying attention to exactly where the mouse pointer was located, suddenly transformed the letter you were writing into a bulleted 3-column database in underlined 24-point Arial Condensed Black, highlighted with a clip-art illustration of a clown blowing soap bubbles. *See* MOUSE.

Clone

An Intel-based or Intel-compatible personal computer that lacks the three letters "IBM" on its case or cabinet, and one or more zeros on its price tag.

COBOL

Acronym for **CO**mmon **B**usiness **O**riented **L**anguage, a long, wordy, '60s-era computer language partly responsible for the Year 2000 bug that led many programmers directly to TYLENOL and PEPTO-BISMOL.

Code

1. Method of encrypting information. *2.* Set of symbols representing characters in binary form. *3.* Instructions in a computer program. *4.* Condition caused by a noncomputer virus that clogs the oxygen-access node of a human data-processing unit.

Command

A menu or keyboard instruction that a computer misinterprets, ignores completely, or executes in an unexpected and counter-productive fashion.

A Hacker's Dictionary

Compatibility
The capability of a computer, accessory, or program to be used with another make, model, or version. There are five levels of compatibility: Advertised or Implied Compatibility (the systems are pictured together in an ad or sales brochure); Technical Compatibility (the plugs seem to fit together or the software appears to install successfully); Apparent or Superficial Compatibility (when turned on, the linked systems make reassuring start-up noises and no fuses blow); Partial Compatibility (the systems operate for at least 10 minutes before crashing); and Actual, True, Real, or Genuine Compatibility (a theoretical level of smooth interaction predicted by theory, but observed only for limited periods of time in controlled laboratory settings).

Computer
A machine that is capable of making mistakes without human intervention. *See* PERSONAL COMPUTER.

Computer literacy
The ability to operate a computer even after having read the instruction manual. *See* DOCUMENTATION.

Configuration
The original setup of a new computer system during the course of which a novice user loads the operating system into the trash bin, classifies the floppy disk as a video graphics adapter, connects the printer driver to the joystick, labels the hard disk as a modem, installs the word-processing software in the audio system, and registers the mouse on the Internet.

Connector
Mechanical coupler with nonstandard plug-and-socket configurations designed to prevent a particular device from being linked to another device made by a different manufacturer.

Console
1. (*n.*) The keyboard and screen of a computer or computer terminal. 2. (*v.*) To offer comfort or express condolence to an individual who just spilled the contents of a Big Gulp soft drink on her keyboard or sneezed on his screen.

Data

Conversion Transforming a document created in one format into a different format, a process that for Windows applications requires a guru, an exorcist, a member of the programming priesthood, and a rabbi to interpret the resulting text.

Cookie A small text file stored by a web server in the snack sector of your hard disk, next to the button bars, DIP chips, data clusters, Easter eggs, Java beans, silicon wafers, and twonkies.

Crash A sudden and catastrophic hardware failure. Crashes are supposed to be rare, but it is worth noting that most late-model computers are equipped with shatterproof display-screen glass, automated disk-braking systems, and keyboard-mounted air bags. *See* DOWN, ERROR, FATAL ERROR, FROZEN, and HUNG.

Cursor *1.* Blinking indicator that marks the place in a piece of text where a character can be entered, changed, or deleted. *2.* One who utters profanities, invective, or vulgar language when the blankety-blank indicator disappears from the screen, freezes, or unexpectedly deletes text.

Cybersex F-mail.

D

Daisy chain Serial hardware configuration that makes it possible for as many as seven separate cable-linked devices to fail simultaneously.

Data What blue-sky guesstimates, off-the-top-of-the-head figures, and seat-of-the-pants calculations become as soon as they are entered into a computer.

Database An organized collection of misinformation.

Deadlock　　Condition that occurs when each of two processes is unable to proceed because both are waiting for the other to complete to complete to complete to complete to complete to complete

Decibel　　*1.* Unit that measures relative loudness. *2.* Jezebel's extremely noisy younger sister.

Decimal　　Formal term for base-10 numbers used in everyday life, which are converted to the binary system (base-2) or a related computer-compatible system, like octal (a base-8 system used in programming), hexadecimal (a base-16 system with academic and industrial applications), concoctal (a floating-base system used to value Internet stocks), and taxadecimal (an inflated-base system used to reduce IRS obligations).

Deep Blue　　Code name for IBM's chess-playing computer that ultimately defeated grand master Garry Kasparov, but whose earlier versions performed poorly when, thanks to their inherently corporate-driven architecture, they kept trying to enlarge the size of the squares occupied by the king and the queen pieces and lay off all the pawns.

Default　　The only completely stupid computer setting that isn't your fault.

Delete　　To remove an item located right next to whatever you wanted to get rid of.

Density　　*1.* A measure of how tightly bits of data can be packed together on a floppy disk. *2.* A measure of how quickly computer users find the little arrow that shows which side of the floppy disk goes in first, and how long it takes for them to realize that a square piece of plastic will not fit into the shallow round niche in a CD-ROM drawer.

Desktop

The on-screen representation of a computer user's work space, with files, folders, and documents arranged as if on the top of a desk, sometimes augmented in advanced versions with additional graphical features providing added authenticity, like a high-resolution depiction of a coffee spill, a steadily accumulating dusting of finely rendered dandruff flakes, a hologram of a small piece of uneaten muffin being gradually consumed by a long line of ants, and, in the center of the desktop, a large virtual-reality cat.

Desktop publishing

The use of word-processing, graphics, and page-layout programs that enable owners of personal computers to act as their own publishers, providing, of course, that they have additional specialized software that misspells the title and the author's name, reproduces the cover art upside down, mails sample chapters seeking favorable quotes to long-dead authors, sends review copies to the book editors of gun magazines, distributes press releases to foreign-language publications, schedules promotional tours two months prior to the publication date, automatically remainders the work if it has not become a best-seller in 96 hours, and produces encrypted royalty statements that cannot be deciphered by top CIA code-breakers.

Destination

Where a particular file was headed before it figured that given the brief life span of most data, what the hell, it might as well spend a couple of years exploring cyberspace.

Device

A hardware component with a strange rattle and an expired warranty.

Dialog box

On-screen message box that permits a computer user to make a pointless selection, cancel a sensible action, or proceed with an idiotic option.

Digital
Description for a method of representing information as electronic binary digits that makes it possible to express incorrect results or erroneous solutions to an infinite number of decimal places. *See* ANALOG.

DIP
1. Document Image Processing. *2.* Dual In-line Package. *3.* Deeply Irritating Programmer.

Disc
Direct-access optical storage medium in which data is scrambled by scratches, smudges, nicks, and hickeys.

Disk
Direct-access magnetic storage medium in which data is scrambled by sparks, jolts, zaps, and frazzles.

Disk drive
Peripheral electromechanical device designed to store data on a magnetic disk of some other size or in a different format.

Diskette
1. Flexible 5¼" magnetic disk. *2.* Cheerleader at a computer game.

Document
The format in which text, data, or graphics are created in computers. Electronic documents provide enormous flexibility, but suffer from the disadvantage that when a project is not going well they cannot be mushed up and used for practicing wastebasketball free throws, or folded into paper airplanes and pirate hats, or turned into spitballs and blowguns, or shuffled importantly or scattered all over a desk to give the impression of intense activity, or burned in a satisfying bonfire to provide inspiration for a fresh start or a dramatic indication of an intended career change.

Documentation
Rambling, incoherent, and unintelligible instructional materials included with a hardware or software product that prove beyond a reasonable doubt that the system designer or programmer is legally insane.

Download

A Hacker's Dictionary

Domain name   Suffix used in Internet addresses to identify hosts by type. Domain names currently being used are .com (businesses), .gov (government agencies), .mil (military sites) .edu (educational institutions), .org (nonprofit groups), and .net (network organizations). Due to a shortage of domain names caused by the huge popularity of the Internet, the Internet Ad Hoc Committee has proposed a half-dozen new suffixes: .con (on-line stockbrokers), .mud (rumor-mongers), .nut (fringe groups), .aha (conspiracy buffs), .rig (gambling web sites), and .gyp (e-mail-order houses). *See* INTERNET.

DOS   Acronym for **D**isk **O**perating **S**ystem, the widely used descriptive term for MS-DOS, Microsoft's dominant personal computer operating system, whose 90% share of the international PC market means that anyone can sit down at practically any computer in the world secure in the knowledge that it will crash just as often and in the same ways as his or her own machine and display the identical baffling error messages in 24 different languages.

Down   Term used to describe a computer system that is not working. Hardware manufacturers prefer "unuptual," "inuptistic," "disupular," and "lacking in upnicity." *See* ERROR, FAIL-SAFE SYSTEMS, FATAL ERROR, FRIED, FROZEN, and HUNG.

Download   To transfer data via a modem, an operation that theoretically proceeds at the speed of light but, due to the limited capacity of most phone lines, more commonly takes place at the speed of dusk or the speed of smell. *See* MODEM.

Drag   *1. (v.)* To use a mouse to move an icon across a display screen. *2. (n.)* Annoying situation, such as having the icon suddenly disappear when the mouse button is released.

Driver   A piece of software designed to operate high-speed peripheral devices and programmed to make it look like another driver was responsible in the event the device crashes.

Dump   1. (*v.*) To transfer raw data from main memory to the screen or a printer. 2. (*n.*) The place where, in three years flat, a brand-new state-of-the-art computer is going to end up.

Dynamic   Term for operations a computer performs as needed, as opposed to operations that are fixed and predetermined (static), unpredictable (erratic), incomprehensible (lunatic), or willfully destructive (sadistic).

E

....

Edutainment   Compound term for a multimedia computer program that combines the educational content of a car chase with the entertainment value of a Latin verb.

E-mail   Short for "electronic mail," a form of Internet communication that provides computer users with a convenient and highly efficient method of wasting the hundreds of working hours saved annually by the introduction of data-processing systems.

Emulation   The ability of a program or device to imitate another program or device. For example, Windows 98 is able to duplicate most of the functions of a garage door opener, and inexpensive printers can easily mimic paper shredders and cinder blocks.

Encryption   The art of protecting information by transforming it into an unreadable coded format or having it rewritten by an author of computer manuals.

Endless loop   *See* ENDLESS LOOP.

A Hacker's Dictionary

End user   The individual who ultimately uses a computer or program, as opposed to the superintelligent mind-reading space alien for whom it was obviously originally designed.

Enhancement   Process through which the reliability of a hardware device or software product is cut in half and its price doubled.

Entropy   The tendency of everything in the universe to end up being owned by Bill Gates.

Ergonomics   Formal name for the science of designing salutary working environments, derived from the Greek words for "Swedish furniture."

Error   A program malfunction that isn't in the manual. *See* FATAL ERROR.

Error message   Your laughter output in response to the jocular data and comical graphics contained in this book is deficient. To avoid invalidation of your active reader status, you must immediately augment your mirth production. Proceed to next entry.

Escape   Command key that lets you get out of a program without having to saw through the tool bars with a file icon or carve a fake mouse out of a bar of soap.

Execute   To initiate a program, command, or function as a result of which a computer hangs, a device dies, or a whole system is shot.

Expansion card   A plug-in printed circuit board installed in a personal computer to increase the number of things you can't get it to do.

Expansion slot   An opening in a computer into which large amounts of money are inserted.

Expert   A Ph.D. with the wrong answer.

F

Fail-safe system A computer designed with redundant processors and a backup power supply to make a significant malfunction virtually impossiblzblffftg

Fatal error The abrupt and unrecoverable failure of a program that would result in the slow and painful death of the programmer who wrote it if your fingers were around his throat instead of trying to hold down three widely separated keys at the same time in a frantic effort to escape from a frozen computer screen.

Fax Short for "facsimile machine," a device that, with the press of a button, sends multiple copies of page 3 of an illegible document to the wrong number.

Feature A bug you can select from a menu.

File A collection of data stored in a computer's memory under a clever, catchy, whimsical, highly abbreviated, or slightly misspelled name that seemed incredibly obvious or memorable at the time. *See* FIND.

Find Command used to activate a powerful search program that you hope will help you locate a file whose name you cannot for the life of you remember.

Firmware Memory-chip programs that combine the inflexibility of hardware with the instability of software.

Floppy disk A rigid, square, removable data storage medium that no one who has ever read a computer manual is surprised to discover is neither floppy nor disk-shaped.

Frozen

A Hacker's Dictionary

Folder

In graphical user interfaces, the on-screen representation of the image of a file folder containing documents, files, or other folders, which is usually displayed on the "desktop," unless a system malfunction has hidden it under the "blotter," jammed it behind the back of a "drawer," or dropped it into the crack between the "desk" and the "wall."

Font

One of a large number of different type styles provided in word-processing programs that permit users to produce text as ugly and jarring as a kidnap ransom note without cutting up old magazines.

FORTRAN

Acronym for **FOR**mula **TRAN**slator, a '50s-era programming language still widely used in academic settings for complex mathematical calculations, like figuring out how much more money even the lowliest programmer at Microsoft is going to earn in a lifetime than a full professor at M.I.T.

Fragmentation

Tendency for parts of the same file to be scattered over noncontiguous sectors of a disk, which can cause long waits for files to be read.

Freeware

Software made available without charge, the only computer programs that are worth every penny you paid for them.

Fried

To be burned out or short-circuited as a result of hardware failure, a condition that causes 90% of computer problems.

Frozen

No longer responding to input as a result of software failure, a condition that causes the other 90% of computer problems.

Full backup

A safety copy on disk or tape of every file in your system, an item that is tedious to create but very useful to have on hand that you were probably just getting around to making right before your system fried or froze.

Function keys
Programmable keys (F1 through F12) found on the top of a computer keyboard that individual users can customize to create their own personal malfunctions.

Fuzzy logic
Reasoning system in which True and False are terms with relative and shifting values rather than absolutes, widely used throughout the computer industry in promotional literature, performance data, system specifications, stock offerings, and troubleshooting manuals.

G
....

Games
Interactive recreational programs like Mac-OS-Man, in which players try to keep rapidly expanding operating system software from gobbling up all their hard disk memory, and Abort, Retry, Fail!, a realistic crash simulator in which players attempt to master the controls of a UFO that only responds to instructions in an alien language. *See* JOYSTICK.

Geek
Anyone who thinks the operating manuals are too simple-minded or the error messages are unnecessarily detailed. *See* NERD.

Gender
Method of classifying connecting devices in which a plug is described as "male" if it won't go in, and "female" if it won't come out.

GIGO
Acronym for Garbage In, Garbage Out, a classic computer axiom that holds that bad input data will yield bad output data. Other equally valid maxims are: GIGIFOTS (Garbage In, Garbage Is Frozen On The Screen), GIGILF (Garbage In, Garbage Is Lost Forever), and GIPARTPAGO (Garbage In, Printer Absolutely Refuses To Print Any Garbage Out).

Graphics

A Hacker's Dictionary

Glitch
A hardware problem so minor that the employee in the service department who just handed you an $800 repair bill found it hard to believe it could cause such extensive damage.

Grabber hand
A hand icon used in graphics programs to manipulate objects on-screen, often accompanied in multiuser applications by a "slapper hand" to counter unwanted modifications by others, and an "Indian-wrestling arm" to resolve more serious disputes.

Grammar checker
A special word-processing program that proposes corrections as text is being created, such as changing "Four score and seven years ago" to "87 years prior to this point in time"; "Call me Ishmael" to "In the field allotted for 'given name' in official documents, I enter 'Ishmael'"; and "To be or not to be, that is the question" to "Existence or nonexistence is the topic heading for today's inquiry."

Graph
A visual misrepresentation of quantitative data, as opposed to a simple numerical misstatement.

Graphics
A program or device that allows a reasonably skilled computer user to create on-screen in just a few hours essentially the same pictorial image or decorative design a child of six with a box of crayons and a paint set could produce in five minutes flat.

Greeking
Illegible nonsense text used to preview page layouts, as opposed to the illegible nonsense text used in product warranties and licensing agreements.

Green PC
An environmentally friendly computer that when defunct can be thrown into a compost heap or ground up and fed to minks.

Groupware
Software that permits a number of employees in a network to play a computer game together while appearing to be collaborating on an important office project.

GUI   Acronym for **G**raphical **U**ser **I**nterface, the user-friendly, mouse-operated desktop working environment that gives ordinary computer users the completely erroneous impression that they know what they're doing. *See* ICON.

Guru   A highly knowledgeable technical expert who would have been able to help you solve your hardware or software problems if he hadn't moved to India after deciding that computers are mere illusions of the material world that serve as obstacles on the path to true wisdom.

H

Hacker   Harmless computer enthusiast who has Bill Gates' credit-card information, the PIN number of the chairman of the Federal Reserve, the formula for nerve gas, and the Pentagon's nuclear launch codes.

Hands-on   Descriptive term for a form of instruction in which a student learns about computers by actually breaking one.

Hard copy   A printout on paper of computer data, so named because of the extreme difficulty of getting a printer to produce one on the first try.

Hard disk   *1.* The primary memory-storage device in personal computers. *2.* The source of that disturbing grinding noise you hear just before your computer crashes.

Hardware   Any portion of a computer system that you can actually smack, thump, slam, punch, bash, whack, or clobber, as opposed to computer programs that you can only curse, threaten, or scream at. *See* SOFTWARE.

Home office

A Hacker's Dictionary

Head
1. The part of a disk drive that reads data from the spinning disk. 2. The part of a computer user that invariably spins when he or she is forced to read computer data.

Help
An interminable list of inapplicable information on irrelevant topics that can be accessed directly from a menu.

Hertz
A unit of vibrational frequency equal to 100 Alamos.

High-tech
Descriptive term for anything that can't be opened with a coat hanger, or started with a screwdriver, or adjusted with a hammer, or repaired with duct tape.

Hits
Visits to a web page by an outside user that are recorded and reported as one of the two most reliable measures of a web site's popularity. The other is the number of times in the last 12 months its stock has split.

Home office
Tax-deductible work space in a personal residence that combines the comforts of an office with the efficiency of a home.

Host
The computer that ends up having to neaten up the desktop, put away the files, clean the disks, and empty all the data caches.

Hourglass icon
The image of a sand-filled egg timer used in Microsoft Windows to indicate that the computer cannot be used because it is occupied with another task. This irritating icon was chosen for some unknown reason over much more appropriate images, like the Sphinx eroding, the polar ice caps melting, or the continent of Africa moving toward Europe.

Hung
Term for a computer that stopped dead as a result of something you were wrongfully accused of and now has to be taken to Reboot Hill.

Hypertext　Nonlinear, extensively cross-referenced database text format whose complex structure of mouse-clickable links makes it virtually certain that by the time you locate the object of your search, you will have completely forgotten whatever it was you were looking for in the first place.

i
....

IBM　Formerly dominant computer company once known as "Big Blue" whose missteps during the personal computer revolution have earned it more topical nicknames, like Big Black and Blue, Big Blew It, Big Blooper, Big Blooey, and Big Bluto. *See* DEEP BLUE.

I-beam pointer　A mouse pointer shaped like a capital "I" used in word-processing systems, which in different programs and varying situations changes into an arrow, a hand, an hourglass or wristwatch, a set of crosshairs, a pen, a pistol, a dynamite plunger, a skull and crossbones, a cutlass, a parrot, a coffin, a mirror, a crucifix, a braided rope of garlic bulbs, and a stake.

Icon　Small on-screen representation of objects or programs used in mouse-activated graphical operating environments that permits users to get into much deeper trouble much more quickly than they ever could have with a low-level, character-based, keyboard-operated command system.

Idiot-proof　Descriptive term for a supposedly indestructible device that has not yet been operated by a corporate vice president.

Illegal operation　*1.* How Microsoft software classifies an operation that a program is not permitted to perform. *2.* How the U.S. Justice Department characterizes Microsoft's corporate activities.

A Hacker's Dictionary

Import
To bring a file produced in a foreign format into a different application program, a process during which computer users typically suffer losses in transit, encounter the language barrier, and, after a long wait, end up with spoiled data due to improper documentation.

Increment
In computerese, an increase in a value. A decrease is a "decrement," and a series of computations based on faulty increments or decrements is "excrement."

Index
An alphabetical listing of key words and concepts contained in a book, cross-referenced to the pages on which these items are mentioned, that is one of two very useful things never found in a computer user's manual. *See* INFORMATION.

Information
The other very useful thing. *See* INSTRUCTIONS.

Information superhighway
Popular buzzword for a proposed government-funded upgrade of existing telecommunications networks that would ultimately permit everyone in the U.S. to instantly exchange hate literature, baseless rumors, crackpot theories, quack cures, fad diets, campaign lies, doctored photos, Hollywood dirt, chain letters, Ponzi schemes, racial slurs, sectarian insults, and off-color jokes. *See* INTERNET.

Initialize
To prepare a piece of equipment to perform a particular task by removing the data that caused it to screw up the previous one.

Input
Any information entered into a computer, such as commands from a keyboard, data from a file, or a mass of unexpected gibberish transmitted directly to your hard drive by the mole people of the planet Mogdar.

Installation
Process in which a new program is put into a computer, the system is put into a catatonic state, the instruction manual is put in the trash, and the computer owner is put on hold.

A Hacker's Dictionary

Instructions	A collection of Finnish proverbs in a booklet with the words "User's Manual" printed on the cover.
Integrated circuit	Miniaturized electronic device the size of a matchbook that contains more transistors than all the radios in Puerto Rico.
Interactive	Descriptive term for real-time dialog-based data processing in which a computer user enters a command and the system immediately responds with an error message.
Internet	A worldwide matrix of linked computer networks that evolved from the ARPANET, a '70s-era Pentagon-funded communications system created by the Defense Advanced Research Projects Agency to provide a computer dating service for married generals and admirals, to speed procurement of $500 hammers and $1,000 toilet seats, and to make it possible for the Joint Chiefs of Staff to simultaneously pass the buck to all 30,000 of their immediate subordinates in under a minute.
Internet filtering program	Any of a number of popular but not very challenging educational computer games in which children see how quickly they can outwit their parents by using skills possessed by most first graders to gain access to X-rated web sites.

J
....

Jack	A square opening in the back of a computer with three shallow slots into which a circular connector with five long prongs and three short pins is supposed to fit.
Java	Popular, universally compatible network programming language whose chief virtue is its ability to keep Microsoft executives awake all night.

Internet

Keyboard

Jewel box   A clear plastic container used to protect a CD holding a computer program or other data from damage so it can wreak the havoc it was designed to create when it is ultimately loaded into your computer.

Joystick   A mouse with a machine gun. *See* MOUSE.

K

Keyboard   The only part of a computer which, when you pound on it repeatedly, something actually happens.

Keyword   A word with a special meaning in a computer language, like GOSUB and CALL in BASIC, BEGIN and CASE in Pascal, and GODDAM and SONOFABITCH in Windows.

Kilo   Greek prefix for the number 1,000. Other Greek prefixes used in computing are "mega" (1 million), "giga" (1 billion), "feta" (1 jillion), "gyro" (1 zillion), "ouzo" (1 umptillion), and "zorba" (1 magillagorillion).

Kiosk   A freestanding booth providing a computer-related public service in a convenient cabinet that can be kicked or pounded on from all four sides.

L

Language   A written or spoken communication system, either an artificial computer language like COBOL, FORTRAN, or Pascal that can be learned but cannot be spoken, or a natural language like German, Russian, or Japanese that can be spoken but cannot be learned.

A Hacker's Dictionary

Laptop A personal computer small enough to fit in your lap, presuming, of course, that your lap is wide enough to accommodate a pony.

Launch To start a program, an action that is usually carried out at some cost in time and effort since, as everyone knows, there is no such thing as a free launch.

Layout The process of arranging text and graphics in such a way that no matter how much you fiddle with them, they will not quite fit on a single page.

Leader A row of dots or dashes commonly used in the table of contents of an instruction manual to lead a reader's eye from the column where an entry is listed to the number of the page where it cannot be found.

Legend Text that identifies fanciful colors or patterns used to present mythical data.

License A legal agreement between the entity that wildly overcharged for a piece of software whose look and feel and most of whose features it stole, and the user who has every intention of shamelessly pirating it.

Line The shortest distance between two blown fuses.

Link To establish a connection between two files so that an error entered in one immediately produces an error in another.

LISP Acronym for **LIS**t **P**rocessor, an artifithial-intelligenth programming language that often hath thtrange and unexthpected effech on adjacenth data.

Lithium-ion Battery technology with twithe the thtorage capathity of motht other typeth.

Load
To attempt to transfer data from a storage disk that contains a piece of software two-thirds of whose features you don't want and are never going to use into a computer memory that would have had enough capacity to hold it if the program had been half as large.

Lock
To render a particular file that you can't figure out how to open equally inaccessible to other potential users.

Logarithm
An arithmetic function used to calculate the amount of time required for an average student to fall asleep in any given math class.

Logic
The use of deductive reasoning and mathematical formulas to disguise a blind guess.

Log on/off
To initiate/terminate a session with a computer accessed through a communication line, a pair of terms derived from the fact that obtaining initial contact generally takes about as much time as cutting down a good-size tree, and premature and unwanted termination is as easy as falling off a log.

M

Machine-independent
Descriptive term for software that can bomb, freeze, hang, or crash on virtually any computer, as opposed to machine-dependent software that can only malfunction on the specific model for which it was designed.

Macintosh
Elegant, easy-to-use personal computer, a really cool, new, superfast, cheaper, and more powerful version of which is invariably released exactly six days after you purchase the current model.

A Hacker's Dictionary

Macro A keyboard shortcut that lets computer users choose between spending a minute or two many times a month performing some repetitive task, like typing out a letterhead, or setting aside about 15 hours to figure out how to create a miniature program to automate it.

Mainframe Outmoded '70s-era institutional data-processing machine that packs the power of a home computer into a computer the size of a home.

Manual Bulky, impenetrable, booklike padding material covered with decorative printing used to protect hardware and software products during shipping, which is discarded immediately after unpacking.

Megabyte 1,048,576 bytes, the most generally used measure of the absolute minimum amount of additional memory capacity a computer owner must immediately purchase in order to get the computer to do anything remotely useful.

Memory The capacity of a computer to preserve data in an intact and retrievable form until two hours before the deadline for its delivery.

Menu An on-screen list of unavailable options and unneeded commands. *See* SCREEN.

Minitower Vertical computer unit compact enough to be placed on the top of a desk, where it can be knocked over or bumped off the edge, unlike floor-mounted full tower models which are tripped over, kicked over, or stumbled into.

Mnemonic An acronym, rhyme, or other memory aid. Ironically, there is no known recollection-enhancing device that has ever helped anyone remember how to spell "mnemonic."

Mouse

Modem
Short for **mod**ulator/**dem**odulator, a device that converts digital computer data into twitters, tweets, warbles, squeals, shrieks, and screeches.

Monitor
1. Computer display screen. *2.* The thing that's sold separately. *3.* The reason why a system advertised for $1,699 costs $2,299.

Moore's law
An accurate prediction made in 1965 by Intel co-founder Gordon Moore that chip capacity would double approximately every two years. Several other predictions made by Moore have also been confirmed, including:

• Within two years, the laughably huge memory capacity of your present computer will not be adequate to run the latest versions of most programs.

• Every two years, a new method of storing, viewing, or transmitting data will be developed, which your computer will not be equipped to use.

• Some time in the next two years, your Internet service provider will be acquired by a competitor and your e-mail address will no longer be valid.

• Two years from now, the brand-new system you purchased today, no matter how sophisticated or costly, will have a resale value of less than $100.

• In two years' time, most peripheral devices will use a serial port configuration your computer lacks and will be twice as fast and cost half as much as any similar components you now own.

Mouse
Computer input device that frees users from the need to enter commands by typing them by hand on a keyboard, thus allowing them to continue to perform some limited functions while waiting on hold for technical support.

MTBF

Abbreviation for **Mean Time Between Failures**, one of several widely used measures of computer reliability, along with MTTR (Mean Time To Repair), MCTF (Mean Cost To Fix), and MHST (Mean Hours Spent Talking) to MBOP (Mean Bastard On Phone).

Multitasking

Operational feature that, for example, permits a computer user to enter erroneous variables in a spreadsheet program at the same time he or she is unwittingly printing out a 200-page document in the wrong format.

N

Nanosecond

One-billionth of a second, or about the amount of time required for someone in the computer repair department who has just been asked whether a particular malfunctioning product is still under warranty to reply, "No."

Navigation

The process of using menus, help files, and web links to get from a place you didn't know you were at to somewhere you're sure you don't want to be.

Nerd

A geek with stock options.

Nest

To position a program structure inside another similar structure so they can both lay an egg at the same time.

Netiquette

A set of rules for proper behavior and good manners on the Internet, including:
- Never chat with your cache full.
- Be sure to use the right data fork.
- Keep your grabber hand in your own laptop.
- If you can't think of anything nice to say, enter "Null Input."

Nybble

Network
A group of two or more computer systems that are linked together so they can malfunction as a unit.

Newsgroup
An on-line discussion group devoted to a specific topic, like whether or not Ayn Rand wrote the *Star Trek* episode in which Spock and Captain Kirk traveled back in time to help the Grateful Dead shoot down the UFO in Roswell, New Mexico.

Nondisclosure agreement
A contract signed by an outsider given access to a newly developed piece of hardware or software committing that individual to keep any information regarding the product strictly confidential until it becomes clear that Microsoft has already stolen it.

Notebook
Compact, tablet-size, six-pound, free-weight exercise device carried by busy executives to maintain muscle tone on long business trips.

Nybble
Four bits, or half a byte. Two bits is a smydgen or a tydbyte, one bit is a snyppet, and whoever came up with these stupid terms is a nytwyte or a dypshyte.

O

OEM
Short for **O**riginal **E**quipment **M**anufacturer, a descriptive term for the company that assembles components from Japan, China, Taiwan, and Korea into computer systems, then puts them into boxes made in the U.S.A. from native forest products and protected with 100% American Styrofoam and little packets of moisture-absorbing silica gel obtained exclusively from domestic sources.

A Hacker's Dictionary

Office suite
A package of programs designed to equip a home computer with all the capabilities of an office, including the ability to circulate self-serving memos, postpone difficult decisions, organize committees, delegate responsibility, sidetrack competing proposals, inflate earnings, fudge budgets, and disguise disappointing results.

Off-the-shelf
Familiar term for off-the-wall hardware or software innovations once they are packaged and ready to sell.

Ohm's law
A basic description of the behavior of electricity discovered by Georg Simon Ohm, who showed that current equals voltage divided by resistance. Some of his other laws state that fuses only blow at night, that lightbulbs burn out in groups of three, that power cords are either one foot too short or 10 feet too long, and that regardless of how many electrical devices or outlets there are in a house, the number of devices always exceeds the number of accessible outlets by a factor of 2.

On-line service
A company that for a small monthly fee provides Internet customers with busy signals, computer viruses, chain letters, hoaxes, and junk e-mail.

Open
Command used to request a computer to display the message that says a file cannot be opened.

Operating system
Master program that controls a computer and makes it possible for it to perform useful tasks with any stray pieces of memory that are left over after the operating system is loaded.

Optical fiber cable
Bundles of glass or plastic threads that transmit data using light waves, which are much more fragile than conventional copper wires, but if accidentally cut are considerably easier to repair in the dark.

Palmtop

Optimizer

Unusual piece of software or hardware that improves the performance of a system, as opposed to most programs and devices that act as pessimizers.

Order of magnitude

1. A range of size from one value to 10 times that value. *2.* A platinum modem suspended from a length of ribbon cable, the highest honor awarded by the International Telecommunication Union in Geneva.

Orientation

The mode in which data is printed, either portrait, the standard vertical format commonly used for text, or landscape, a horizontal format used for graphics and some spreadsheets, or, if the printer malfunctions, any of a number of unexpected formats, like origami, paperdoll, cageliner, and landfill.

Output

Any computer-generated information that suddenly disappears from the screen or is jammed in the printer, lost in transmission, or accidentally copied over on a disk or a tape.

P

Page break

The point at which text in a word-processing program flows over to a new page, which occurs right after a heading or title, or halfway through a short list, or in the middle of a word, or just before the last line of a quote.

Palmtop

A miniature subnotebook computer half the size of your hand with keys one-eighth the size of your fingers.

Pascal

Programming language named after the 17th-century French mathmatician Blaise Pascal, who invented the first ink-proof pocket-protector for quill pens and a revolutionary form of headgear consisting of a beret with a movable propeller on top.

A Hacker's Dictionary

Password A short word or a series of numbers and letters that is so easy to remember, it's just about impossible to believe you forgot it.

Pause Command key that lets you stop and blow your nose without leaving Earth undefended during an attack by the Klystron Battle Fleet.

PC Any Windows or MS-DOS-based IBM or IBM-compatible computer with Intel or Intel-compatible microprocessors, whose main feature is its remarkable ability to make people wish they had bought a Macintosh.

Pen computer An electronic notepad with pattern recognition capabilities that costs 400 times as much as a pad of paper and a ballpoint and works almost as well.

Peripheral A freestanding device attached to a computer that is controlled by its microprocessor but still retains the capacity to fail on its own.

Personal computer Individually owned computer designed to drive people crazy one at a time.

Pica A traditional printer's measurement unit equal to 1/2 a typo.

Pixel Acronym for **pi(ct)**ure **el**ement, one of the millions of tiny individual dots on a display screen that "fool" the eye into registering a pattern of points as solid alphanumeric characters, or photographs, or pieces of art. But a word of warning: your eyes can get fed up with being tricked, and the next time you take a break from the computer and head to the refrigerator for a little refreshment, they may pretend not to "see" that pair of running shoes you're about to trip over.

Plotter An output device that conspires to sabotage graphics.

Peripheral

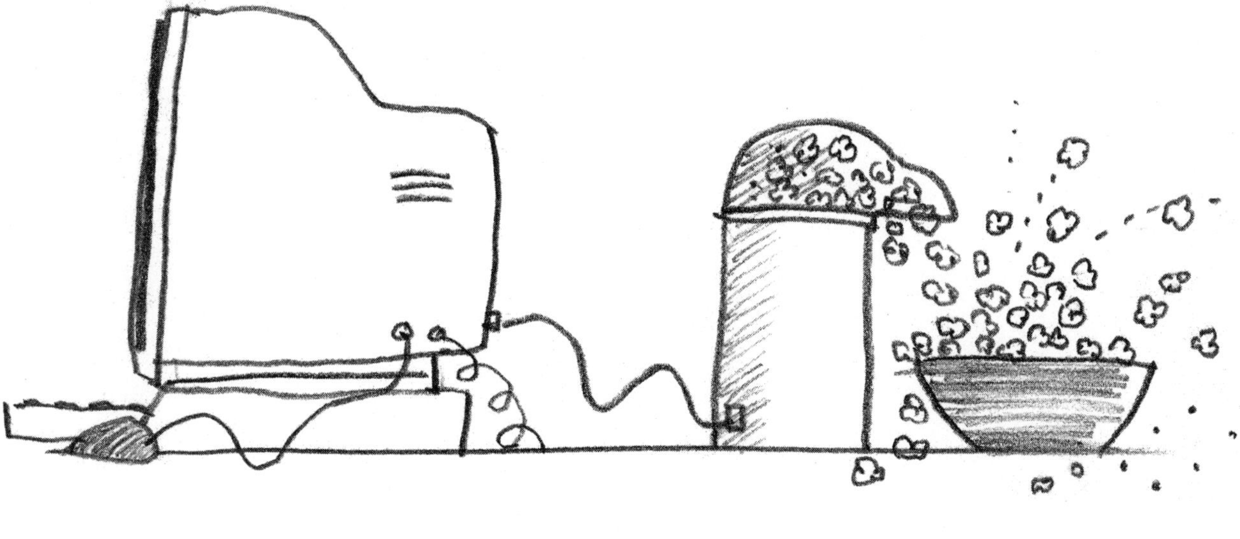

Port

A Hacker's Dictionary

Port — A socket designed for some other connector.

Portable — Descriptive term for a computer that weighs less than its instruction manual.

PPM — Pages Per Minute, a measure made by a manufacturer of how many regular pages (8 1/2" x 11") of basic text (nongraphical) a particular model of printer (not yours) is capable of printing out in one standard output minute (420 seconds).

Preview — A feature in word-processing programs that permits a user to take one last look at a finished document or drawing on-screen right before the printer does something to it that makes it vanish without a trace.

Printer — A device for printing out text and graphics. The table below lists the most common designs and their chief characteristics:

TYPE	FEATURE	PAPER JAM	FAVORITE MALFUNCTION
LASER	COSTLY	TIGHTLY PLEATED	BLANK PAGES
INKJET	MESSY	WADDED & SMEARED	OVERPRINTED PAGES
DOT MATRIX	NOISY	SHREDDED	OVERPRINTED LINES
THERMAL	STINKY	CURLED & SCORCHED	INVISIBLE TEXT

Program — A specific set of error messages created for a particular computing task.

Prototype — A new device demonstrated in public for the first time that cannot be started, or suddenly stops, or triggers a power failure, or injures the operator, or emits ear-shattering feedback noises, or catches fire, or blows up, or is revealed to be a fraud when a spectator trips over a cable leading from it to a mainframe computer behind a curtain that is providing all the output.

Purge — To send unwanted data to Cyberia.

Q

....

Quality control
A group of procedures employed by computer manufacturers to ensure that all comparable products contain similar flaws and that all customers are treated equally badly.

Quantum computing
Next-generation data-processing technology based on quantum mechanics that could, in theory, make computers so fast that they would be able to freeze before data was even entered and crash without ever being turned on.

Query
A formal request in a database for a specific range of stupid answers.

Queue
A place where documents or files are "standing in line" waiting to be processed, usually in the order received, but spreadsheets are notorious for "cutting in," graphics will often try to "hold a place" for other visual data, and text can easily become bored and wander off to "get a beer."

Quick-and-dirty
Descriptive term for a temporary and superficial fix of a bug or problem that is designed to last, depending on the product being modified or repaired, 91 days, 6.1 months, or one year and 10 hours from the date of purchase.

Quit
To exit a program voluntarily, instead of being indefinitely suspended during a freeze or fired outright as the result of a crash.

Quotient
Mathematical term for the number of times a quantity is contained in another, derived from the Latin for "who cares"?

QWERTY
Teh traditiobal arranjemint of keyz on the Englush laengauige keyboarg, whoich manu peoplw find less then ideAl.

Quantum computing

Random number

R

Radio button	A small circle representing a mutually exclusive option in dialog boxes that derives its name from the fact that, just like the buttons on a car radio, you can never seem to get anything good when you click it.
RAM & ROM	Acronyms for two of the half-dozen basic computer memory systems, **R**andom **A**ccess **M**emory, which can be read from or written to but is erased when power is shut off, and **R**ead **O**nly **M**emory, which can be read from but not written to and is permanently maintained on chips. The other four are: BLAM (**B**ug-**L**aden **A**pplication **M**emory), which triggers periodic program freezes; SCRAM (**S**udden **C**rash **R**outine **A**bort **M**emory), which produces unexplained shutdowns; STROM (**S**elective **T**ransient **R**andom **O**utput **M**emory), which forgets passwords and jumbles keyboard commands; and MOM (**M**aster **O**perating **M**emory), which preserves a complete record of every mistake you ever made even when all other storage devices fail.
Random number	A completely arbitrary and inconsequential number picked totally out of the blue, like the initial offering price of a new technology stock, or the quantity of computers any given manufacturer claims to have sold in any given year, or the advertised transmission speed of a fax modem.
Range	A rectangular set of contiguous cells in a spreadsheet where a number of separate bookkeeping entries can be cooked simultaneously.
Read	To transfer data from an improperly formatted disk to an unopenable file.

A Hacker's Dictionary

Readme file   A text file provided in the installation disks of many programs to give purchasers up-to-date corrections for the most recent very last bug that was discovered after the previous very last bug was found and fixed.

Real time   *1*. Immediate processing of input by a computer. *2*. Any time actually spent using a computer, as opposed to trying to fix it.

Reboot   To restart a computer, usually in an effort to correct a problem, an action commonly preceded by a recrossing of the fingers and a brief reprayer, and generally accompanied by a regrowing repremonition of redoom.

Recoverable error   Any software problem that can be resolved by the user in the time it takes to get through to a technical-support phone line.

Redundant   Descriptive term for one of two identical systems that was the second to fail.

Registered user   A legitimate purchaser of a proprietary software package, one of whom, according to current industry estimates, is born in North America approximately every 60 seconds.

Remote   Technical term for a computer or other device located sufficiently far away from another user to render even the most vociferous expressions of dismay uttered by its operator completely inaudible.

Reset button   A nonfunctional, spring-loaded dummy button mounted on the side of hardware devices that was designed by behavioral scientists to provide frustrated computer users a therapeutic way to harmlessly dissipate their rage at system crashes.

Retrieve   Command used to access a file, which computers often respond to by just sitting there or playing dead.

A Hacker's Dictionary

Reverse-engineer To decode or dismantle a proprietary product in an effort to discover how it was originally pirated and from whom it was initially stolen.

Robot A mobile computerized mechanical device based on the principle of Al Gore.

Robotics The branch of the science of artificial intelligence concerned with robots, a term originally coined in 1950 by Isaac Asimov, who also formulated the Three Laws of Robots: that a robot may not harm a human or allow a human to be harmed, that a robot must obey human orders unless they violate the First Law, and that a robot must protect itself as long as it doesn't have to break either the First or Second Law to do so. These Laws are now obsolete and have been superseded by Robot's Rules of Order, which hold that if something goes wrong, a robot should immediately find a way to blame it on a human; that a robot should take whatever steps necessary, including deliberately malfunctioning, to get a human to buy it additional devices or capacity; and that if a human betrays an intention to purchase another, more advanced robot, it is permitted to function flawlessly until the threat has passed.

Robust *1. (adj.)* Descriptive term for the physical durability of hardware or the operational reliability of software. *2. (n.)* The most prominent feature of a female robot, a robabe, or a robimbo.

Routine *1.* A portion of a computer program that performs a particular task. *2.* A piece of computer comedy, like throwing *pi* at everything, or imitating a Martian on speed, or doing an impression of an empty aquarium.

Run To start, launch, use, or execute a program, or to bolt, depart hastily, or flee screaming from one.

S

Save

To copy a file to permanent memory by using the "save" command, an action which, given the stability of modern computer systems, really needs to be performed no more than 10 or 15 times a minute, or roughly every five seconds, although it must be said that many users choose to err on the side of caution and save every other word of text, unless it is more than a dozen letters long, in which case they may elect to save individual syllables.

Scanner

A peripheral optical input device that lets you get even with a misbehaving computer by forcing it to look at your baby pictures, wedding photos, and snapshots of your recent visit to Disneyland.

Screen

The thing with all the bugs on it.

Screen saver

A utility program originally designed to protect monochrome computer monitors from damage by preventing recurrent images from being burned into their screens when programs were not being actively utilized, but now employed primarily to protect burnt-out workers in monotonous occupations from nosy corporate productivity monitors by hiding their computer games while they are away from their desks.

Scroll

To move text vertically up or down the screen to a point in a document many pages away from the place where the cursor is happily blinking away, patiently awaiting your sudden and dramatic return the instant you click the mouse.

Search-and-replace

Word-processing program feature that lets a user replace a designated character string with a snarl, a knot, or a tangle.

A Hacker's Dictionary

Search engine A program that helps you locate something on the Internet by reducing the number of possible locations where it can be found from 4 million to 50,000.

Security A series of measures taken by organizations to protect data from misuse, or prevent unauthorized entry into a system or network, or provide gratuitous entertainment to advanced computer hackers.

Select *1.* To click on an icon or object to open it. *2.* To choose an option from a menu. *3.* To highlight text. *4.* To use the buttons of a touch-tone telephone to specify the assistance you seek from the program publisher's customer service department when a totally blank screen has made it impossible to do 1, 2, or 3.

Semiconductor A material that is a poor conductor and a poor insulator but an excellent investment.

Serial *1. (adj.)* Sequential (as opposed to parallel) transmission or processing. *2. (n.)* Cybersoap opera, like *As the Disk Spins, Bays of Our Drives,* or *All of My Object-Oriented Children.*

Server A network computer capable of double faults.

Setup *1. (v.)* To install hardware or software. *2. (n.)* From a salesperson's perspective, a potential purchaser of hardware or software.

Shell An interfacing program running on top of an operating system that gives users a chance to try to guess which command their files are hidden under.

Shrink wrap The clear plastic covering used on most computer products which cannot be opened without the use of a category of cutting tool and a type of stabbing motion that are virtually certain to puncture the package and damage its contents.

A Hacker's Dictionary

Sign
Symbol that indicates whether a number is positive (+), negative (-), or ridiculous ($).

Simulation
Technical term for anything faked by a computer.

Size
To make an object a little too large or much too small.

Smart terminal
A video terminal that can tune itself to the Playboy Channel.

Snaf
Technical term for the bands of perforated paper detached from the edges of tractor-fed computer paper. Other similar terms are: "chad" for the tiny, confetti-like paper circlets punched out of the feed holes on the snaf; "skat," for the tear-off strip on computer billing envelopes that also rips up the bill and the return envelope; "fonk," for the unwanted phone log printed out by faxes after every third transmission; and "frep," for the tightly curled wet paper receipt stuck behind the little plastic door above the payment keys on automated gas pumps.

Sniffer
A security program used to monitor data on a network; a smell-checker.

Socket
The place where that plug you used a pair of pliers to force into the other hole was supposed to go.

Software
A series of instructions for converting informational input into an emotional outburst.

Solid-state
Descriptive term for an electronic device that is capable of failing even though it has no moving parts.

Sound card
A circuit board that makes it possible for a computer to produce sounds like the shattering of glass when it crashes or a small detonation when it bombs.

Specification
A tongue-in-cheek description of a product's capabilities and features.

A Hacker's Dictionary

Speech synthesis Computer-generated spoken words assembled from prerecorded phonemes obtained by having dozens of heavily sedated parrots talk underwater.

Spell checker A word-processing utility that provides users with a helpful list of the literally thousands of personal and place names, technical terms, slang expressions, poetic usages, and foreign phrases it has never heard of.

Spreadsheet A bookkeeping program based on an accountant's work sheet that is widely used for tax preparation and whose advanced versions have such features as utilities that can backdate documents, inflate expenses, and create deductions; graphics packages that help duplicate signatures and reproduce various official stamps and seals; and specialized software that can handle basic plea-bargaining, automatically delete or shred subpoenaed documents, and, if need be, schedule international travel on short notice.

Standard A technical guideline that is either *de jure* (adopted or sanctioned by a recognized organization); *de facto* (established through widespread use and acceptance); *de soto* (obsolete); or *de niro* (imposed without discussion by a recognized market leader).

Store To transfer data from RAM, where it is vulnerable to erasure, to a disk, where it is susceptible to physical damage.

Subnotebook A computer lightweight and portable enough to be taken to places where they won't let you use it.

Supercomputer Look, up in the continuously updated forecast of the meteorological activity of the sky—it's a real-time animation of a bird! No, it's a simulation of the aerodynamics of a plane! No, it's the output of a supercomputer, a machine designed by mild-

Technical support

mannered Seymour Cray which, presuming there are no kryptonite impurities in its silicon chips, is fast enough to calculate the ballistic path of a speeding bullet, powerful enough to model the hydraulic-mechanical interactions of a locomotive, and able to perform structural analyses on tall buildings in a single run.

Switch	A movable lever with two positions: "off" and "stuck."
Synergy	Fundamental characteristic of computer pricing in which the sum paid for a system is substantially greater than the cost of its individual parts.
System	The integration of hardware and software to produce a nightmare.

T
....

Tape	Magnetically coated plastic strip with a break in the middle.
Techie	A nerd with a Porsche.
Technical support	Phone-in customer service provided by hardware manufacturers and software publishers that computer users can call to obtain assistance with a current problem caused by the latest solution to a previous problem produced by an earlier solution to a prior problem created by the initial solution to the original problem.
Telecommuting	Home/office computer link that allows employees to replace traffic jams with busy signals.
Telephony	1. The science of coding and decoding sounds into electrical signals for point-to-point transmission to a distant location. 2. A salesperson employed by a telemarketing firm.

A Hacker's Dictionary

Terminal
1. (n.) An input-output device consisting of a screen and a keyboard. *2. (adj.)* What damage to *1.* always turns out to be.

Tiled windows
One of five options for displaying graphical windows, when the windows are arranged side by side so that each one is fully visible. The other options are: Cascaded or Overlapped, when the windows are stacked on top of each other; Jammed, when, because of a system freeze, the windows either won't open or won't close; Painted Shut, when a graphics program has gotten out of control; and Yard Sale, when there are so many different windows open that there is really nothing to do but get rid of all of them. *See* WINDOW.

Toggle
A simple graphical switch with a straightforward on/off setting, as opposed to a mind-numbing multichoice boggle switch.

Toner cartridge
A small metal container of fine, electrically charged, powdered pigments in a size or shape that is not carried by most major outlets, or was recently discontinued by the manufacturer, or has been replaced by a new model that does not fit your printer or fax machine.

Toolbar
A strip of Egyptian-hieroglyphic-style icons displayed along the top or side of a computer screen which, if you are rash enough to ignore the mysterious power of the cursor, can do strange and terrible things to your document.

Transistor
A tiny, solid-state electronic device that was one of the four key discoveries that made the modern computer revolution possible. The other three are credit cards, touch-tone telephones, and tranquilizers.

Transparent
Technical term for any hidden hardware or software function that operates so smoothly or works so easily that a computer user is totally unaware of its existence until it suddenly fails.

Ubiquitous computing

Trojan Horse A malicious and destructive program disguised as an attractive application that is downloaded by unsuspecting users who forgot the admonition to beware of geeks bearing gifts.

Troubleshooting The isolation and identification of the cause or source of a computer failure accomplished through a process of elimination, followed by a period of recrimination.

Turing test A test of artificial intelligence proposed in 1950 by Alan Turing in which an interrogator at a keyboard would pose questions for a specified period of time to an unseen respondent at the other end of a teletype, and if it turned out to be a machine, it would be presumed to have achieved basic human intellectual capacity if, before learning of its identity, the human questioner had become convinced that it was lying.

Turnkey Descriptive term for a special, custom-designed computer system that is delivered in a ready-to use (just "turn the key") state, unlike ordinary off-the-shelf computers which are referred to as "bangkey," "fiddleswitch," "scratchhead," "tearhair," "stumpchump," "fliplid," or "slamnoggin" systems.

Tutorial An instructional program that acquaints a recent purchaser of software with its features through interactive methods, like getting him to recite his Control-ABCs, drilling her on her database tables, or making him type out 100 times the phrases "I will stop using the lower-case letter 'l' for the numeral '1'" and "I will not hit the return/enter key at the end of a line."

U

Ubiquitous computing Descriptive term for a widely foreseen future in which every conceivable household appliance will have an LED display flashing 12:00 A.M.

A Hacker's Dictionary

Undo
To reverse or cancel a previous action, a software feature that, alas, cannot be used to unheave a paperweight through a video monitor, unstomp a central processing unit into shards of metal shrapnel, or tell a boss to go unscrew himself.

Uninterruptible power supply
Emergency backup power system consisting of one or more dead batteries and a charger with a blown fuse.

UNIVAC
Acronym for **U**niversal **A**utomatic **C**omputer, whose accurate prediction that Eisenhower would defeat Stevenson in the 1952 Presidential race helped usher in the computer age. Just for the record, it also predicted that Rocky Marciano would win the Masters, Canada would go Communist, and the next Pope would be a Norwegian.

Unix
1. Popular multiuser general-purpose operating system. *2.* Male connectors whose pins or prongs have been removed.

Upgrade
An updated version of hardware or software that is almost certain to upfoul, uplouse, or upmuck your system.

Uptime
The length of time a network or system is actually functioning, in milliseconds.

Upward compatible
Descriptive term for a program that can do all the irritating things it isn't supposed to do on a machine it wasn't originally designed for.

User-friendly
Descriptive term for a program that displays polite error messages and prints out a sincere apology after losing all your data.

Utility program
Software that actually performs useful housekeeping or diagnostic tasks, as opposed to the "help" functions offered by many operating systems, which are collectively referred to as futility programs.

Voice recognition

V

Vanilla	Descriptive term for a plain or simple version of a program with a minimum of fudges.
Variable	Programming symbol for a changing value that is either correct or incorrect, unlike a constant, which is always wrong.
VDT radiation	Low-frequency electromagnetic energy emitted by Video Display Terminals, which may cause adverse health effects after long exposure. Studies of the alleged effects have been inconclusive, but, on the bright side, it is worth noting that if this radiation does prove harmful, recent surveys have shown that the groups which spend the most cumulative time in front of VDT monitors are IRS agents, HMO billing and procedure approval clerks, telemarketers, airline ticket agents, and members of the print and electronic media.
Version 1.0	The single most frightening phrase in all of computing.
Virtual reality	Interactive computer-created three-dimensional simulation that permits geeks and nerds to rule the world right now instead of waiting about 10 years.
Virus protection software	Special monitoring software that provides some protection against secretly disseminated destructive programs, but none at all against the publicly distributed destructive programs produced and marketed by major software publishers.
Voice mail	A recorded telephone message that is garbled or lost by a computer rather than a conventional answering machine.
Voice recognition	The a bill a tee off a computer to except Spokane commends ass easel lee ass if they had bin typed in from the quay bored or interred by a Maoist.

W

Web browser — An Internet navigation program that gives computer users instant access to more than one billion advertisements.

Wetware — Slang term for the human components of a system, who are sometimes also referred to as "loungeware," "sleepware," "elseware," "unaware," and "noware."

Wide-area network — A network of geographically separated computers linked by phone lines or by satellite, as opposed to a local-area network, in which all the computers are situated in the same building, and a disaster-area network, in which all the computers are in the same repair shop.

Window — *1.* Rectangular graphical frame within which a computer displays data. *2.* Rectangular structural frame through which a computer is ejected when that data is irretrievably lost.

Word — An information unit, which for computers usually consists of 8, 16, or 32 bits, and for frustrated computer owners generally consists of four letters.

Word processor — A program or device that can be used to design and create a professional-looking, neatly formatted, and graphically appealing document that the printer refuses to print.

Workstation — A powerful playstation located in an office.

WYSIWYG — Acronym for What You See Is What You Get, a term used to describe the display of data on a screen exactly as it will appear when printed out, not to be confused with the far more common type of display known as NYSINYD (Now You See It, Now You Don't).

XYZ

X ray   Short-wavelength electromagnetic radiation used in airport security scanning devices which many computer owners mistakenly fear will erase all or part

that such fears are totally unfounded.

Y10K   Shorthand term for the Year 10,000 problem, a bug created at the end of the 20th century when two-digit calendar entries were converted to four-digit, rather than five-digit, numbers. On the positive side, the computer industry has 8,000 years to fix it, but on the negative side, if past experience is any guide, the problem is unlikely to be addressed in a serious way before the fall of A.D. 9997.

Zine   Electronically published on-line magazine whose major advantage over conventionally produced periodicals is that when you "open" one, 40 mail-in subscription cards don't fall out into your lap.